ROCKFORD PUBLIC LIBRARY

3 1112 01557497 9

☝ **W9-BJL-439**

J 932 STR
Strom, Laura Layton
Tombs and treasure :
ancient Egypt

**030508**

**ROCKFORD PUBLIC LIBRARY**
Rockford, Illinois
www.rockfordpubliclibrary.org
815-965-9511

SHOCKWAVE
SOCIAL STUDIES

# Tombs and Treasure

## Ancient Egypt

© 2008 Weldon Owen Education Inc. All rights reserved.

No part of this publication may be reproduced or transmitted
in any form or by any means, electronic or mechanical,
including photocopying, recording, taping, or any information storage
and retrieval system, without permission in writing from the publisher.

Library of Congress Cataloging-in-Publication Data

Strom, Laura Layton.
  Tombs and treasure : ancient Egypt  / by Laura Layton Strom.
      p. cm. --  (Shockwave)
  Includes index.
  ISBN-10: 0-531-17787-4 (lib. bdg.)
  ISBN-13: 978-0-531-17787-7 (lib. bdg.)
  ISBN-10: 0-531-15478-5 (pbk.)
  ISBN-13: 978-0-531-15478-6 (pbk.)
1.  Egypt--Civilization--To 332 B.C.--Juvenile literature.  I. Title. II. Series.

  DT61.S92 2007
  932--dc22

2007010017

Published in 2008 by Children's Press, an imprint of Scholastic Inc.,
557 Broadway, New York, New York 10012
www.scholastic.com

SCHOLASTIC, CHILDREN'S PRESS, and associated logos are trademarks
and/or registered trademarks of Scholastic Inc.

08 09 10 11 12 13 14 15 16 17
10 9 8 7 6 5 4 3 2 1

Printed in China through Colorcraft Ltd., Hong Kong

**Author:** Laura Layton Strom
**Educational Consultant:** Ian Morrison
**Editor:** Janine Scott
**Designers:** Avon Willis and Carol Hsu
**Photo Researcher:** Jamshed Mistry

**Photographs by: Getty Images** (p. 16; p. 20); © **Hunterian Museum & Art Gallery, University
of Glasgow** (p. 15); **Ingram Image Library** (pp. 8–9); **Jennifer and Brian Lupton** (teenagers,
pp. 32–33); **John Hunt** (p. 30; view of Cairo, p. 31); **Ian Massam** (Valley of the Kings, p. 17);
© **The Trustees of the British Museum** (p. 29); **National Geographic Image Collection** (p. 11);
**Photolibrary** (cover; p. 15; Ramses VI's tomb, p. 17; mummy of Ramses II, p. 18; p. 28;
ship on the Suez Canal, p. 31); **TopFoto/www.stockcentral.co.nz** (cat mummy, canopic jars,
pp. 18–19; p. 25); **Tranz/Corbis** (p. 7; Hatshepsut, p. 15; p. 21; p. 23; pp. 26–27)

The publisher would like to thank John Hunt for the use of his photographs on pages 30 and 31.

All illustrations and other photographs © Weldon Owen Education Inc.

SHOCKWAVE
SOCIAL STUDIES

# Tombs and Treasure

## Ancient Egypt

Laura Layton Strom

ROCKFORD PUBLIC LIBRARY

children's press®

An imprint of Scholastic Inc.

NEW YORK • TORONTO • LONDON • AUCKLAND • SYDNEY
MEXICO CITY • NEW DELHI • HONG KONG
DANBURY, CONNECTICUT

# CHECK THESE OUT!

Stuff to Shock,
Surprise, and
Amaze You

Quick Recaps
and Notable
Notes

Word Stunners
and Other Oddities

The Heads-Up
on Expert Reading

Links to More
Information

# CONTENTS

**afterlife** a life or an existence that some believe follows death

**amulet** (*AM yuh liht*) a locket or other object worn to keep away evil

**archaeologist** (*ar kee OL uh jist*) a scientist who studies people and objects from the past

**hieroglyphics** (*hy roh GLI fix*) a system of pictures and symbols that stand for sounds, words, or ideas

**mummy** a dead body that has been preserved

**papyrus** (*puh PYE ruhss*) a paper-like writing material made from a reed-like water plant

**pharaoh** (*FAIR oh*) a ruler of ancient Egypt

**pyramid** (*PIHR uh mid*) a massive monument with a square base and four triangular walls, with inner burial chambers

· · · · · · · · · · · · · · · · · · · · · · · · · · · · · · · · · · · · · · · · · · · · · · · · · · · · · · · · · · · · · · · ·

For additional vocabulary, see Glossary on page 34.

In this book, the word *pyramid* refers to a large monument with a square base and triangular sides. This kind of monument is named for its shape. In math, however, a pyramid can have different-shaped bases, such as a triangular base.

Egypt is a country in northeast Africa. **Ancient** Egypt was one of the earliest organized societies in the world. About 6,000 years ago, small towns and cities grew up on the banks along the great Nile River. These ancient cities became famous centers of trade. Ancient Egypt was ruled by **pharaohs**. Egypt became a rich and powerful nation in the ancient world.

We know ancient Egypt best for the grand **pyramids** built as tombs for its rulers, and for the **mummies** that were found in those pyramids. However, ancient Egyptians left many other great achievements.

Great Sphinx

Ancient Egyptians invented a form of picture writing. They also invented a paper-like writing material. They were clever architects, engineers, and traders.

The Great Sphinx guards the pyramids at Giza near Cairo, Egypt.

## ANCIENT EGYPT

| | |
|---|---|
| First semipermanent villages along Nile River | 4500 B.C. |
| Earliest picture writing | 3100 B.C. |
| The Great Pyramid built at Giza | 2560– 2540 B.C. |
| Egyptian rulers buried in the Valley of the Kings | 1550– 1100 B.C. |
| Reign of Queen Hatshepsut | 1479– 1458 B.C. |
| Reign of Tutankhamen | 1347– 1339 B.C. |
| Reign of Ramses II, Egypt's greatest builder of temples | 1290– 1224 B.C. |

The numbers representing B.C. years decrease as we count forward in time.

9

# The Black and the Red

The Nile River runs through Egypt. People began to live along the Nile thousands of years ago. The river provided water for life. Every year, the Nile flooded. It washed thick mud over the riverbanks. It left good soil behind. Ancient Egyptians called this soil the "black land."

A short journey from the banks of the Nile led to desert in all directions. The ancient Egyptians called the red sand "deshret." That means "red land." Where the black land ended, the red land began. A person could stand with one foot on **fertile** ground and one foot on hot, dry sand.

Mediterranean Sea

Alexandria

Giza · Cairo

Giza Pyramids

Great Sphinx

Nile River

Red Sea

Valley of the Kings

EGYPT

Abu Simbel

This map shows some of the monuments built during ancient Egyptian times.

Farm laborers grew crops such as wheat, barley, and onions in the black land. Oxen plowed the land. Goats trampled the seeds into the soil. The laborers worked for the pharaoh or wealthy landowners. They were often paid in wheat and barley.

Along the Nile River, a person can easily see the black land and the red land.

Red land

Black land

Here is a hot tip to help you spell the word *desert*. Would you like a second helping of sand or ice cream? The *dessert* we eat has two helpings of the letter *s*. *Desert* has only one *s*.

# A River of Three Seasons

Life in ancient Egypt depended on the Nile River. The river was like a great roadway. People used the river for transportation and trade. They fished in its waters. They hunted waterbirds along its banks. The river supplied water for drinking and washing too.

Every year, the people waited for the river to flood. If it didn't flood, there would be **famine** in the land. Because of the river, the farmers' year was divided into three seasons. From July to October, the river flooded, so farmwork stopped. From November to February, farmers plowed and sowed. Harvesttime was between March and June.

Fish was an important food for ancient Egyptians.

The Nile was used for:
- transportation
- trade
- food
- drinking
- washing

The farmers plowed the soil. Then they sowed the seeds.

At harvesttime, the farmers reaped the crops.

People raised water from the river with a **shadoof**. They watered the crops.

13

# The God-Kings

For about 3,000 years, Egypt was ruled by kings and queens called pharaohs. Most pharaohs were men. Sometimes women were pharaohs too. Pharaohs wore fake beards tied to their chins. Even the female pharaohs wore fake beards.

The people of Egypt believed that pharaohs were god-kings. The god-kings took part in many ceremonies. They built temples to their favorite gods. They built temples to themselves. The pharaohs' lives and deeds were recorded on the walls of their temples.

Hmmm. The first sentence discussed the word *pharaoh*. I can be pretty sure that the rest of this page will be all about pharaohs.

# Meet Some Famous Pharaohs

**Hatshepsut:** First woman pharaoh. Hatshepsut took over in 1479 B.C. All descriptions about her as pharaoh were chipped off carvings or painted over.

Hatshepsut

**Tutankhamen:** Famous for his burial treasures. King Tut became pharaoh at age 9. He died in 1339 B.C. at about age 19, perhaps murdered by his **successor**. His tomb was discovered in 1922.

**Ramses II:** Known as Ramses the Great. He was famous for building great monuments, such as the Abu Simbel temples.

Cleopatra VII

**Cleopatra VII:** Famous for being the last Egyptian pharaoh. Cleopatra killed herself by making a poisonous snake bite her.

Ramses II

Cartouches (below) show the name or symbol of a pharaoh. They have helped **archaeologists** understand the picture writing on the temple walls.

15

# Pointed Tombs

Ancient Egyptians had strong beliefs about what happened after death. They believed they needed their bodies in their next life. When pharaohs died, they believed they went to live with the gods. So a pharaoh's body needed to be kept safe. For many, only the biggest, strongest tomb would do – a pyramid.

The building of a pyramid took thousands of workers. Each stone block was heavier than a small truck. Pyramid builders had no modern moving or lifting gear. Gangs of workers moved the stone blocks with the help of shadoofs, sledges, and wooden rollers.

More than two million stone blocks make up Khufu, which is also called the Great Pyramid.

By 1550 B.C., pharaohs thought that their bodies and treasures would be safer hidden in tombs cut from rock in the desert. A rocky gorge near a pyramid-shaped mountaintop was chosen as the burial place. It is called the Valley of the Kings. Sixty-two tombs have been found there.

Inside Ramses VI's tomb

Today, many tourists visit the Valley of the Kings.

Pyramid-shaped mountaintop •

• Tombs

• Tombs

# Mummies of Egypt

It was a mummy maker's job to preserve dead bodies. This took about 70 days. It was an expensive process. Only pharaohs and the wealthy could afford it. Mummy makers first removed the vital organs. They stuffed the body with sand or sawdust, then dried and **embalmed** it. Finally, the body was wrapped in linen strips and put in a coffin. Many mummies were buried with food, drink, clothes, and wigs for their journey to the **afterlife**.

Mummies offer us a look back in time. Archaeologists can figure out the age, health, and diet of a mummified person. Sometimes they can even tell how they died.

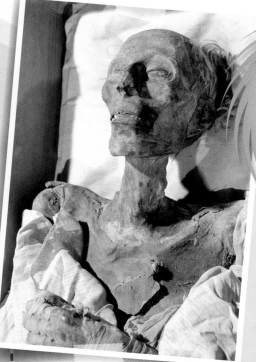

SHOCKER

Mummy makers first removed the body's vital organs. The brain was pulled out through the nose, using a hook. The brain was thrown away!

The body's vital organs were put in four sealed jars, called canopic jars. They were placed in the tomb. The heart was left in the body. It was needed to get into the afterlife.

Liver          Lung

Lid of outer
mummy coffin

Lid of inner
mummy coffin

Mummy
with mask

Some Egyptians
mummified their pet
cats. Mummies of dogs,
monkeys, and crocodiles
have also been found
in tombs.

Base of inner
mummy coffin

Base of outer
mummy coffin

Stomach     Intestines

Steps for preserving
the dead:

1. Remove vital organs.
2. Stuff body with sand
   or sawdust.
3. Dry the body.
4. Embalm the body.
5. Wrap the body in linen strips.
6. Put the body in a coffin.

19

# Buried Treasure

A pharaoh's tomb was filled with treasure. Mummy makers often wrapped precious jewels and lucky **amulets** between the mummy's wrappings. Sometimes they placed eyes made from **gold leaf** over the body's eye sockets.

Of all the pharaohs' tombs, the greatest find was the tomb of Tutankhamen. It contained fine gold jewelry, gems, statues, and sculptures. It had games, furniture, clothes, and weapons. There was even a golden **chariot**!

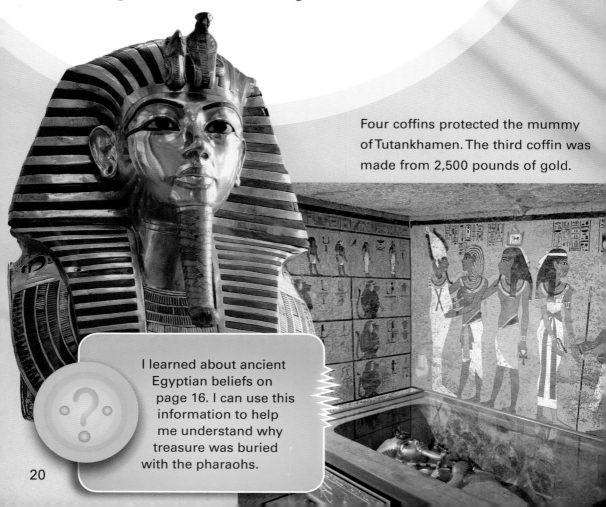

Four coffins protected the mummy of Tutankhamen. The third coffin was made from 2,500 pounds of gold.

I learned about ancient Egyptian beliefs on page 16. I can use this information to help me understand why treasure was buried with the pharaohs.

Robbers raided many of the tombs. They stole the treasures. They even destroyed some of the mummies. To fool robbers, pyramids were often built with false doors, false passages, and fake burial chambers. The pharaoh's chamber was also sealed with large blocks called sealing plugs.

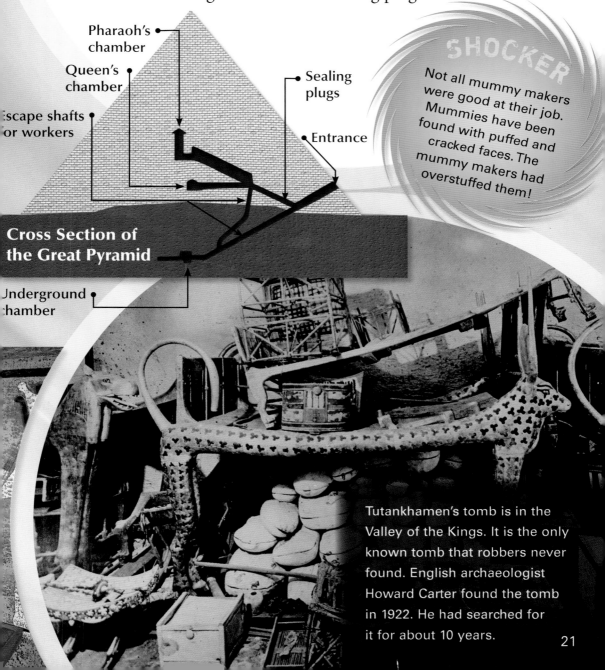

Pharaoh's chamber

Queen's chamber

Escape shafts for workers

Sealing plugs

Entrance

**Cross Section of the Great Pyramid**

Underground chamber

SHOCKER

Not all mummy makers were good at their job. Mummies have been found with puffed and cracked faces. The mummy makers had overstuffed them!

Tutankhamen's tomb is in the Valley of the Kings. It is the only known tomb that robbers never found. English archaeologist Howard Carter found the tomb in 1922. He had searched for it for about 10 years.

21

# Ancient Messaging

Much of what we know about ancient Egypt comes from the information carved or painted on the walls of the tombs and temples. These walls are like history books. They are a record of the deeds of the pharaohs and the people of that time.

The ancient Egyptians used pictures instead of an alphabet like ours. This form of picture writing is called **hieroglyphics**. Each picture, or hieroglyph, represents a letter, sound, or word. The hieroglyphs could be written from left to right or right to left. They could also go from top to bottom.

**Scribes** were the only people who could read and write hieroglyphics. They used **hieratic writing** for recording information on **papyrus** scrolls. This form of writing was quicker to do than hieroglyphics.

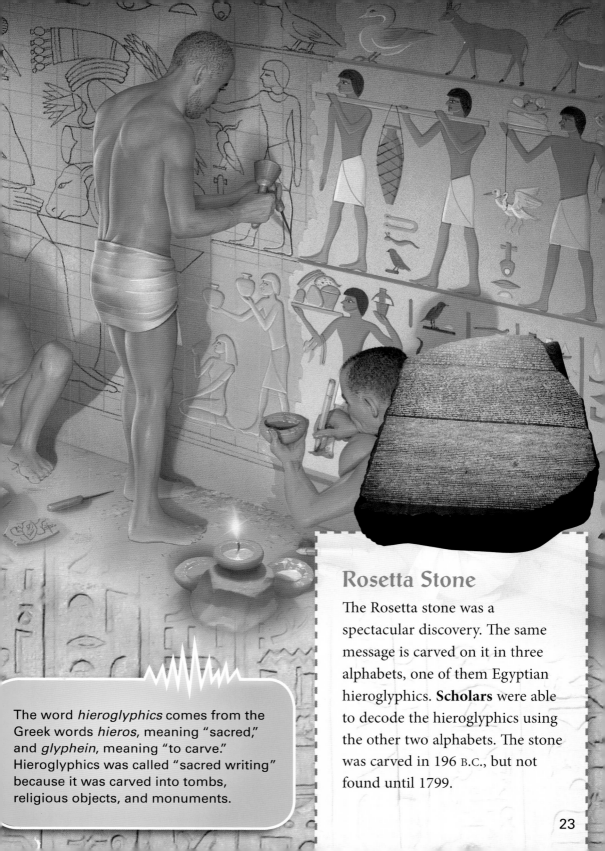

## Rosetta Stone

The Rosetta stone was a spectacular discovery. The same message is carved on it in three alphabets, one of them Egyptian hieroglyphics. **Scholars** were able to decode the hieroglyphics using the other two alphabets. The stone was carved in 196 B.C., but not found until 1799.

The word *hieroglyphics* comes from the Greek words *hieros*, meaning "sacred," and *glyphein*, meaning "to carve." Hieroglyphics was called "sacred writing" because it was carved into tombs, religious objects, and monuments.

# Ancient Foods

The main food of ancient Egyptians was bread made from wheat. Many people ate vegetables, fruits, and fish. They drank mostly beer that had very little alcohol. It was made from barley.

An Egyptian marketplace had many different goods. Ancient Egyptians didn't use money. People brought things to market to swap for what they needed. Stallholders weighed produce against copper weights, called debens.

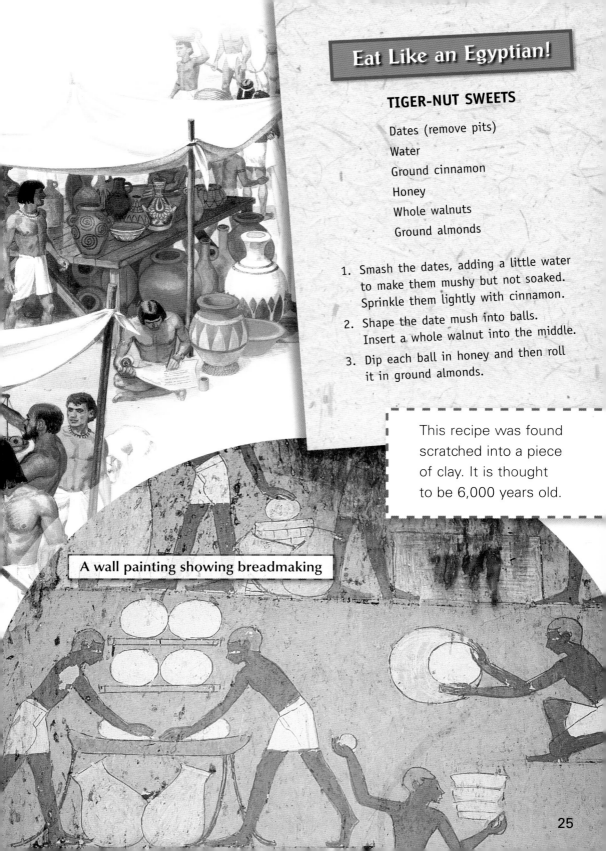

## Eat Like an Egyptian!

### TIGER-NUT SWEETS

Dates (remove pits)
Water
Ground cinnamon
Honey
Whole walnuts
Ground almonds

1. Smash the dates, adding a little water to make them mushy but not soaked. Sprinkle them lightly with cinnamon.
2. Shape the date mush into balls. Insert a whole walnut into the middle.
3. Dip each ball in honey and then roll it in ground almonds.

This recipe was found scratched into a piece of clay. It is thought to be 6,000 years old.

**A wall painting showing breadmaking**

# The Social Pyramid

Ancient Egyptian society was shaped like a pyramid. It was divided into three main classes. The pharaoh ruled Egypt and was at the top of the pyramid. High priests, government officials, and scribes were part of the upper class. Craftworkers made up the middle class. Farmers and laborers were at the bottom of the **social pyramid**. They made up the lower classes.

Scented cone of animal fat

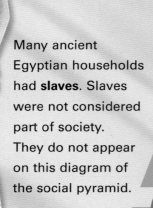

Many ancient Egyptian households had **slaves**. Slaves were not considered part of society. They do not appear on this diagram of the social pyramid.

Pharaoh

High priests

Government officials

Scribes

Craftworkers

Farmers and laborers

Ancient Egyptians were buried in areas according to their place in society. The pharaohs were buried in a valley. The paintings on the walls of their tombs tell us much about the lives of the different classes. From these paintings, we know that wealthy Egyptians wore wigs. They decorated themselves with jewelry. The men and women drew black eyeliner around their eyes. Farmers and laborers wore a cloth skirt around their waist.

Wig

Black eyeliner

**SHOCKER**

No party costume was complete without a cone of perfumed animal fat on the head. The cone was lit as the men and women entered the party.

Wealthy Egyptians used shiny bronze or copper as mirrors to check their reflections.

# Family Life

Most people in ancient Egypt lived in villages. The villages had mud-brick houses with flat roofs. There was little furniture inside the houses. Chairs were a sign of importance. All homes had statues of the household gods. Many families had pets, such as cats, dogs, birds, and monkeys.

Ancient Egyptians lived short lives. Thirty was old age! Because of this, girls and boys married when they were between twelve and fifteen years old. Wealthy boys went to scribe school to learn to read and write. Most children worked alongside their parents.

Boys and girls had toys, such as spinning tops, balls, and dolls. Adults played board games.

### Ancient Egypt
- very little furniture
- age 30 very old
- married by age 15
- toys were homemade

### How We Live Now
- much more furnitur[e]
- age 30 not old
- in school at age 15
- toys and games often bought

City houses in ancient Egypt often had several floors. The homes of poor people usually had only one room. The homes of the rich had as many as 70 rooms!

Statue of an ancient Egyptian house

SHOCKER

When a pet died, the whole family shaved off their eyebrows. This was a sign of sorrow.

In ancient Egypt, balls were made from leather. Children also had wooden toys. Some toys could be pulled along on wheels.

# Egypt Here and Now

Today, Egypt is still a powerful country. There are no pharaohs. Egypt is a **republic** led by a president. In 1869, the Suez Canal was completed. It links the Red Sea to the Mediterranean. Today, taxes on ships passing through the canal are one of the two main sources of income for the Egyptian government. The other is tourism.

Many people work in the tourist industry. Some are guides who take people to see the ancient tombs and temples. Some people make goods and sell them to tourists. Other people work in hotels and on the many tourist boats that sail on the Nile River.

There is a lot of information here, but I can use the photographs on these pages to help me understand what I am reading.

In Egypt, school is free from age six. Many children take school trips to learn about their ancient history.

More than 76 million people live in Egypt. Many Egyptians are very poor. Most Egyptians live in large cities, such as Cairo and Alexandria. Some live in small villages along the Nile. They farm the land in much the same way as ancient Egyptians did. Today, the Aswan High Dam controls the flow of the Nile River. There are no floods to bring fertile mud. Farmers use fertilizer on their land instead.

Cairo is the capital of Egypt. It is a large, busy city. Air pollution is an enormous problem in Cairo.

Donkeys and horses still play an important part in Egyptian life. They transport people and goods.

Ship on the Suez Canal

Mediterranean Sea

Suez Canal

Great Bitter Lake

Little Bitter Lake

Red Sea

...two temples at Abu Simbel, built by the pharaoh Ramses II 3,000 years ago, are among the most magnificent monuments on Earth. To complete the Aswan High Dam, a huge lake was planned that would submerge the temples. The Egyptian government, with the help of UNESCO, launched a worldwide appeal to save the monuments.

## WHAT DO YOU THINK?

Is the money spent on taking care of ancient structures a good use of money?

### PRO

I think we need to preserve the past for the education of people now and those in the future. We've learned a lot from what the ancient Egyptians left behind.

Between 1964 and 1968, the two temples were dismantled and shifted, piece by piece, more than 190 feet up the sandstone cliff. The cost of the project was $80 million. The moving of the temples is considered one of the greatest engineering feats in archaeology. The two temples are a UNESCO world heritage site. They are visited by millions of tourists each year.

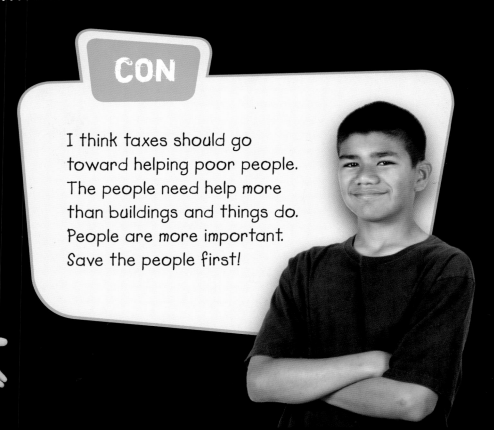

**CON**

I think taxes should go toward helping poor people. The people need help more than buildings and things do. People are more important. Save the people first!

# GLOSSARY

**ancient** (*AYN shunt*) very old or from long ago

**chariot** (*CHA ree uht*) a small, two-wheeled vehicle, pulled by a horse, used in ancient Egyptian times

**embalm** (*em BAHM*) to preserve a dead body so that it doesn't decay

**famine** (*FAM uhn*) an extreme shortage of food

**fertile** (*FUR tuhl*) full of nutrients that help plants grow

**gold leaf** gold that has been beaten into very thin sheets

**hieratic** (*hye RA tik*) **writing** a simplified script form of Egyptian hieroglyphics

**republic** a country controlled by a government and its president, not a king or queen

**scholar** (*SKOL ur*) a person who specializes in a particular area of study

**scribe** (*SKRIBE*) a person who copies documents by hand

**shadoof** a pole with a bucket and a weight, used for lifting

**slave** a person who belongs to someone else and must do whatever that person tells him or her to do

**social pyramid** a triangle showing the most powerful people at the top and the least powerful at the bottom

**successor** a person who takes someone else's job when he or she finishes it

Chariot

# FIND OUT MORE

## BOOKS

Challen, Paul C. *Life in Ancient Egypt*. Crabtree Publishing Company, 2004.

Haslam, Andrew. *Ancient Egypt*. Two-Can Publishers, 2001.

Rossi, Renzo, and Salmeri Pherson, Anna Maria. *The Egyptians*. Barron's, 1999.

Sands, Emily. *Egyptology Handbook*. Candlewick Press, 2005.

Strom, Laura Layton. *The Egyptian Science Gazette*. Scholastic Inc., 2008.

Woods, Geraldine. *Science in Ancient Egypt*. Franklin Watts, 1988.

## WEB SITES

Go to the Web sites below to learn more about ancient Egypt.

www.ancientegypt.co.uk/menu.html

www.historyforkids.org/learn/egypt

www.kidskonnect.com/AncientEgypt/EgyptHome.html

www.egyptologyonline.com

http://touregypt.net/kids/Life.htm

# INDEX

# ABOUT THE AUTHOR

Laura Layton Strom is the author of many fiction and nonfiction books for young readers. She has worked as an educational writer, editor, and publisher for more than 20 years. Laura loves Egyptian history. She was among the first to buy a membership at her city museum when she heard the King Tutankhamen exhibit was coming to Chicago. She encourages all readers to visit their local history museum.